God, Seed

ALSO BY REBECCA FOUST

All That Gorgeous Pitiless Song (Many Mountains Moving, 2010)

Mom's Canoe (Texas Review Press, 2009)

Dark Card (Texas Review Press, 2008)

ALSO BY LORNA STEVENS

Huia (Trillium Press, 2006), altered book, edition of twenty

God, Seed

Poetry & Art About the Natural World

Rebecca Foust and Lorna Stevens

TEBOT BACH * HUNTINGTON BEACH * CALIFORNIA * 2010

Cover art: *Dandelion,* watercolor by Lorna Stevens
Frontispiece: *Seed*, drawing by Lorna Stevens
Graphic design: Lorna Stevens and Jeremy Thornton
Author and artist photograph: Jeremy Thornton

Royalties from this book will be donated to the David Brower Center in Berkeley, California, home to organizations working for environmental and social justice.

ISBN – 10: 1-893670-47-3
ISBN – 13: 978-1-893670-47-1

Library of Congress Control Number: 2010928291

Poetry, Poetry and art about the natural world, Poetry --21st Century

A Tebot Bach book

Tebot Bach, Welsh for little teapot, is a Nonprofit Public Benefit Corporation which sponsors workshops, forums, lectures, and publications. Tebot Bach books are distributed by Small Press Distribution, Armadillo, Ingram, and Bernhard DeBoer.

The Tebot Bach Mission: advancing literacy, strengthening community, and transforming life experiences with the power of poetry through readings, workshops, and publications.

www.tebotbach.org

Printed in Canada on FSC Certified papers and with vegetable based inks by Printcrafters, an FSC Certified printing company. All paper waste, plates and press chemicals used in the making of this book have been recycled in a responsible manner.

*This book is dedicated to the natural world
and to the hope that we will learn
to be better stewards of it.*

CONTENTS

I

II

III

I

GOD, SEED

God   seed
sprout   shoot
root   stem

bloom
womb   fruit
blight

hand of man
gourd and husk
famine   dust

ash   loaves
of stone   rain
rain and rain

sun, then
sea cedes
to land

a fish head feeds
each mound.

LAKEMONT PARK

The crickets are sounding a catastrophe
outside my window, reminding me
of the painted tin clickers whose tongues

we'd arc and release, consolation prizes
for the perennially rigged ring toss,
that huge stuffed orangutan getting more

moth-eaten every year, smell of sweat
and hot axle grease, gear eating gear when
the paint-peeling rolly coaster creaked

its way up and plunged past the carousel,
the real crickets' jig-chorus racket
in the long-limbed grass where we spread

our thin blanket. Then the carnival light
and crackle would fade, then I'd arc
and release again and again. Your hands,
your tongue, the cricket-sung, grass-sweet dark.

NOW

I remember your archipelago spine, nape of knee,
inner ankle secret spot, instep arch,
places in the body's uncharted waters, new worlds
lying green and deep off winter's bow

and now, spring. Bone-ache thaw, wind sough
through snow-scoured woods, bud swell
on bare branches, birdsong and blossom
and all that cruel choir of memory and desire

sung into the air's dredged honeycomb. Warm
wax and pollen, semen, and slept-in sheets.
Lunch boxes and laundry in prism. Something
unfolding its wet wings in bloom.

SONOMA OAK TREE

Knee-deep in owl clover,
wild mustard, white
firework wildflower.

Three kinds of fern:
maidenhair, sword,
Japanese painted.

Galleon-girth trunk
twisted back — a god
caught surprised.

MOUNT ELLINOR HIKE

Avalanche lilies blooming in snow,
hikers with boards on their backs,
my delight in the ice axe

you put in my pack. Bear grass in bloom
— who knew it did anything
but bend slender stems

in suburban floral arrangements?
Deer sausage thick as my thigh
from the buck you shot last year.

The extra gear you made me bring,
which I disdained but quickly
layered on when we summited

in a whiteout blizzard. On descent,
the dislodged rock ricocheting
down   down   down

just past my head. Above on
the ridge the goat with her kid,
chewing a meditative cud.

DAWN POPPIES

When night opens throat
in frog and cricket call,

the buds are blunt, blind
fingertips, candle ends.

Origami stars unfold
and at dawn fold up again.

When sun ascends
soprano sky, the silver web

is seared, and sepals split
to flame

illegal red. A child's wail
blooms.

CHERRIES

Her mouth is crammed
with the fruit
she'd climbed the low
branches to pick
in the old T-shirt
she wears sometimes
for her nightgown.
She sucks the stones
to bare bone, then spits.

Her feet are bare
and stained red,
her lips
are stained red,
her lips are jammed up
next to his thighs
so close she can just
barely part them.
Like this. And this,
like an eyelash kiss,
oh like this.

A QUESTION

Was pleasure
ever given
more succulent flesh
than in this first bite
of sun-ripened tomato,
Brandywine, Cherokee
or yellow cherry, picked
warm from the vine
in a garden that smells of
the earth's own wine cellar
—sweet mulch, sorrel
and sunlight
churned by the bees
into curds of thick,
thyme-scented honey?

WINDFALL APPLES

I've eaten my fill
of windfall apples,

pippins picked
by wind, softened

by sun into brown
apple butter.

I've piled my basket
with tonguetart,

poutpucker, mouthwater
Winesaps,

green Grannys, Galas
in harlequin

yellow, streaked red
where sun

has lain, juicy
with rain.

POMEGRANATE

Half the world for a round, red
pomegranate, heavy as stone,
four-lobed
leathery globe.

Compact, jampacked with seeds,
each udder-taut universe
encased in what shapes
a raindrop.

Community of seeds with weight,
white-felted, honeycombed
cobbed-corn ruby rows.
Persephone

tried to resist, but when she bit
into that pellucid explosion,
she filled her mouth with it,
red-wine-distilled light.

OCTOBER

The summer sun like a fist
striking your forehead
now become blessing and balm,
a palm lightly laid on your brow,
and now you can smell
the pungent complexity of bay
crushed underfoot with the thick,
watermarked leaves of live oak.
Light slants down in shafts
making a pollen radiance
of a black-tarped mudslide
you once mistook for God.
The trees hold the last light
like votives. No fog, but a vapor
smudges the crowns
of the redwoods and ridgelines
of Mt. Tam. Toyons erupt
in tawny, bunched berries
cedar waxwings get drunk on, and sing.

PERSIMMONS

So useful in metaphor: better
to pick the fruit from the tree than wait
for its fall to the ground,
and the way leaves wither away,
leaving behind what counts,
poignant winter tableaux,
bare boughs bending with fruit.

But best is the way in this case at least
ripeness really is all, and it is the young flesh
that is shrewish, too tightly set, too tart
to eat, absurdly acerbic, bitter,

while the mature persimmon,
even wrinkled, even withered, even sunk
to deliquescence of melt
is luscious flesh, youth
only a green trace bitterness
on the roof of a mouth otherwise palated
with rich river pudding, plush and pulp,
soft-slide swallow delight
and sweet, sweet.

PERSIMMONS II

She sat at her desk; outside
the tree greened,

then glowed dull yellow
and let go

its leaves. Birds swooped
and dove

in a riot of ripe, rotting fruit
and sometimes

looked in at her. She closed
her eyes and when

she looked out again, it all
was gone.

II

UNHEARD

A *marvel of unicorns* or
a *herd of wild
bison,* what might
be called a Lazarus
species, thought
bygone but somehow
miraculously
reborn.

An *impossibility
of puffins,* now
bittersweet irony,
but a *route
of wolves*
foretelling
its own dire truth,
like the correct term
of venery
for huia and dodo:
an *extinction of* —

a plenary erasure. Of
their bones are fossils
made, flesh
and blood seen
no more by my child's

child,
nor touched,
nor heard,
nor even heard of.

FOSSIL RECORD

Brachiopod, trilobite,
ammonite, crinoid stem,
fern in stone with spores
strung like pearls along
each bract, snakeskin
tree bark, imprint wing
pressed and fanned; one
metatarsal wears a ring.

Substrate less self,
negative space
embraced by stone
womb, corpus luteum.
What has and what will,
pre- and post-virginal
version of *be,* preamble
and postscript of *am.*

Thick wedged slate,
old X-ray plates,
dense and dark,
shot through with light,
exposing heart,
the inner part of things —
what's been unveiled,
what's been enshrined

in sunken shaft
of mine or light,
bones thrown down
of czar or thief,
of bird or wife.

RAYSTOWN RIVER TROUT

It took my hook like kite-caught wind.
I had to fight to reel it in, to net
its taut dense-bodied surge, heft
and heave of oiled writhe.

I knew about the upstream mine,
uncapped and seeping mercury, so I
wore gloves to hold the fish no fool
would eat and waited for the mystery

and passion. There was no *rainbow,*
rainbow, rainbow, no communion
with Christ's flesh. Just this prism
flash gone gray and my sick wish

not to have caught it; I wished I'd cut
the line before the glitter got away.

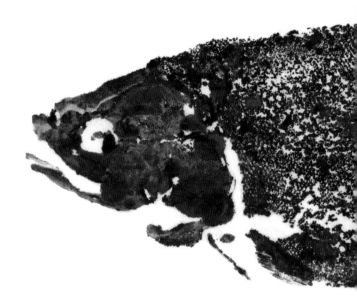

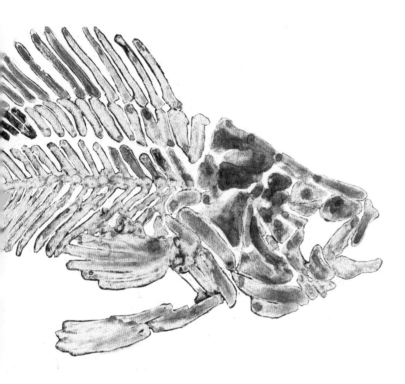

LISTEN

to the slow, savage seep
of earthly beauty, cricket
cadence swelling soft dusk,
rain-stick stutter of seeds
incanting a monsoon memory,
its long, slow surge.

Wade waist-deep into a lake
in equal parts wet and white
moonlight. Meaning: the light
comes from neither water
nor moon, but reflects
a reflection. Unbolted satin
shimmers pale furlongs,
less sui generis than the idea
of itself; homage to homage,
song to mirage, to mist recalling
its past as water brimming
a great, ancient ocean,

the mystery of Fibonacci's
crystalline series, of diatoms
fletched and fluted
like snowflakes, of one
pale, pink, whiskered fish.

THE CORMORANT

[Satan] flew, and on the Tree of Life... / Sat like a Cormorant...
— John Milton, *Paradise Lost,* Book IV

The four-chambered heart and wings
somehow transcend his reptilian brain
and come with dusty black feathers

that fray the frock coat of this dour,
penurious parson. An oddly dense
puddle of shadow inking the float,

he does not deign even one glance
in our direction. We dog-paddle close,
but he waits until we touch wood

to unfold awkward, creaking wing,
splash down on water, upend, dive
and, sleek as a snake, disappear,

no ripple or wake. We climb up, cold and late. The sun
in decline has turned the lake red. It's already starting to burn.

SECONDARY POISON

I.
We spray our roses
for aphids
eaten by songbirds

who, after the poison
has penetrated
the matrix,

begin to lay
eggs empty as if
sucked out by foxes,

or with shells
too thin to contain
the embryo,

broken yolk
dried like spit
on the asphalt,

and one day
only crows left
to sing sunrise.

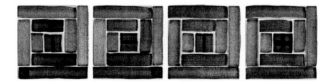

II.
Mice eat d-CON
stored in the shed
by someone

a decade ago
and don't die
right away,

but weaken,
fall prey to owls
or kittens

like this one
at our front door,
lying next to

the delicate, coiled
rose of her feces,
purged beyond purge

beyond purge, eyes
still glittering green.

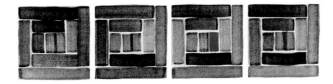

DAY

Each day at dusk, a man
drove his old truck
to the barn to shoot

the magpies he'd trapped
in a cage there. Asked why,
he said *because I can,*

and when he used Malathion
in that green valley,
every last songbird died

in one light-dappled morning, in
one-tenth of a day.

BEE FUGUE

Something's wrong — some pesticide, parasite, or virus
infecting the honeybee brain —

the workers fan out in dawn beelines, mucking
chest-deep in pollen, forcing French kisses

from flowers, but by dusk they are looping zigzags,
gone off plumb, can't find

their way home to the hive. Their thigh sacs are heavy
and ache to draw comb, but

some template's been changed. Each saturate drop
that thickens the comb, the pheromone sillage

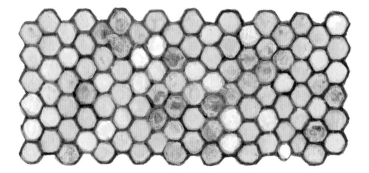

of the sultry queen —these things remain. What's lost
is the way back, which train

or track through the blank blue sky. The hive must be
starving, that is if it's still there

and not like the others gone silent and withered. Empty
of worker, or queen, or drone,

but still crammed with capped brood and uneaten food.
The robber bees are keeping their distance,

even the carnivorous mites. Nature's imposed her stone
quarantine, and who will pollinate the grain?

We are enmeshed in our interconnectedness, betrayed
by our genes. This is what extinction means.

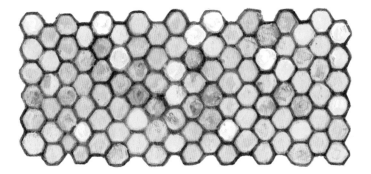

LOVE CANAL

Little life, blighted bud,
limbs unperturbed by
single
breath,
blue, translucent, still.

Here end those months
of waiting while I
nourished you, lying
on my left side, drinking
cisterns of water.

I stilled my fears, called
back my heart
from its full-moon howl
so you, little comma,
would not be afraid.

I willed my womb
to hold you close,
a cradle that became

your ferry across the dark river
before you saw light.

SPILL

didn't they say the PCBs
had not got into Slough Pond
still pure as April   didn't

they plug the leak   the babies
before him born perfect
on time   without

the hysterics of surgical tray
forceps and hand pump
weren't they perfect   rolling

yes   rolling, crawling
and walking
in that order   reading

left to right   letters not
cutting line like children
turned away on purpose

so you can't see what's
written on their faces
didn't they say they'd

plugged the leak   that
he'd not lost too much blood
that they'd clamped

the cord   stopped the bleed
before the PCBs sickened
the groundwater

didn't we remove our clothes
and plastic-bag them
buy new shoes

sign the waiver
didn't we release them
from blame   didn't we

release them   didn't we

FROG

Trapped in the pail
the frog slow-arced
in backflip,

two extra legs
half-folded, flapping
like unbelted umbrellas.

The radio said the PCBs
had not seeped into
Slough Pond.

It's true that nature
not-meddled-with
makes her mutations

routine as breakfast
and does not deem
them tragic.

Still, sleeping,
I dreamt of my son,
his genes expressed

not as autism, but as
four thumbs on two
extra hands

and I want to blame
someone. I want
to drain that pond.

NUCLEAR

My country, O my Ilium, home of the gods,
Golden-arched womb and first assembled UN,
O all-protecting glorious battlements
And Star Wars Defense Systems
Of Troy! Four times as it is moved, it halts
And we ignore gravity's warning, ignore natural law
At the city gates, and four times then there is
Every hour struck on the doomsday clock.
Within the horse the sound of armor clashing,
Threshed atoms, matter gnashing its teeth.
Yet blind with fury and not knowing what
Lives will be uncreated, not knowing what
It is that we are doing, we keep going.
We keep going not knowing, not knowing
Until we have enshrined the monstrous Thing
With its cartoon fins and Hollywood graffiti,
In the very citadel itself. Cassandra is there,
Kin with Oppenheimer who keens
And even then cries out in prophecy,
Now I am become Death. I am become
Of the doom that was right now coming upon us,
I am become Death, the destroyer of worlds,
But by a God's command his voice was never heard,
By a god's command her voice was never
To be believed by Trojan ears. And we,
Blinded by *the radiance of a thousand suns,*
Unhappy people, on this our final day,
Gaze up at the gods of science, kneel, pray, and
Festoon the town with celebratory garlands.

TELEOLOGY

In the seed lies all that it can ever be,
shoot, plant, flower, fruit and
in the end again, the seed.
In the acorn, the entire tree.

One quark encrypts a universe,
a world unfurls from just one joule
of fire. An atom splits and spews
Japan. Blood, bone, gene, cell

predict events as well as tell them,
and no science, god or creed can
crack the code, unwind the strands
that bind our eyes and blind our hands.

We walk a land that's charted. Even as some war
ends somewhere, somewhere a war has started.

HERCULANEUM

Crouched in the garden's
dark corner

sense signals sense signals
sense

heavy air head press heat
burned breath

mouthnosemouth ash petal
thicksift

tremor dread before sound
roar borne down

mud wall mud sea mud world
and womb

when it comes we're already
entombed

LAST BISON GONE

Ours is the curse of the blighted touch
that wilts every green shoot and flower
we mean to admire, keep, re-create

or improve. New Zealand's huia bird,
prized for her scimitar beak
and pleated Victorian petticoat tail,

was hunted extinct except for this
diving-belled brooch and sad hatband,
fast falling to dust

in the Smithsonian. We love what we love
in the scientific way, efficient, empiric,
vicious, too much

and always we touch it, our breath
blooming algae on the walls of Lascaux,
shimmering in acid-etch green.

AFTER

She thought it was snowing
but it was only the world

turning to ash; she wished
it were cold

so she could see otherwise
how thickly

the trees were curded along
each branch,

the rubble confectioned,
sculpted

and stiff-peaked like beaten
meringue,

the silence so precisely
conscripted.

III

RECEIVE

Sit without thought & receive
what is offered:

a curtain of motley drawn
by the weeping cherry,

one slantwise birch clutching
its last pale yellow leaves,

as many shades of green as
places to look,

gray lichen on a fat clay pot
lobed like a pumpkin,

an iron bench, spare & wrought
as punctuation

& you not part of this picture.

SEEDS

of the giant sequoia
come cone-born, encased
in diamond-hard coats;
something secreted
encrypts them against
climate and time
lets them wait out
the cold-ground
generations of winters
for that lightning-crack
thunderbolt trunk-split of fire
that will fissure them to life.

Dull glitter of years
layering down. But when
the firestorm comes,
the ground melts and boils
like stew, swelling each seed
from germ to koan,
seeking meaning
from rain, memory
from pain, how it feels
to feel anything.

UPRISING

A visitation of vultures attended Dad's
death, and Mom's flashed a dark, distant
wing from somewhere above my heart,
beak-picked, grown cold with watching

her make good radiation fodder, lungs
shredded to gauze, mouth one oozing
sore. My tear ducts, vestigial, resorbed.
Long patient roost in the brush,

sleeping and waking in dry, feathered
darkness. Until many molts later,
the pulse that beat on the monitor:
Here   I'm here   Here   I'm here

in the four-celled heart of my embryo son.
Then came the rifleshot, air-crack buckle
of stone made flesh. The birds lifted
their black hearts in crescendo, and left.

I'LL SING YOUR BONES

the bits left sifting ash, tang
of sharp char in the air,

your bones, your teeth, the earth
that they mix with, the loam,

leaf mold and topsoil, the bone
oil smear in smoke

smudged across sky. I'll sing
alum, the scraps of you

eaten by worms, translating dirt
into light, I'll sing

your elixir drunk by the roots
of the jonquils, I'll sing

where it's evergreen in the thrust
through the sky of the pines.

I WANT TO FEEL

what trees do,
leafing out
in June,

the moon
ascending
its light-ladder,
the sun at
equinoctial noon.

I want to feel
what earth does
when it turns
over after winter
and breathes,

water under
crack of thaw
when light
shafts through
canyon wall,

stars, when stars
release all
five frozen
points,
and fall.

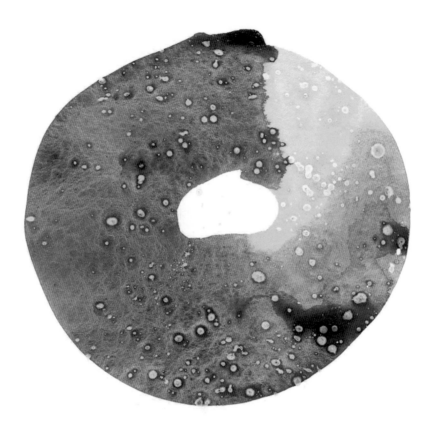

PLUNGE

on eating a Wellfleet oyster

Heavy as stone,
tiny sealed tomb—

clamp-lid tried
pried, then levered—gives.

Knife severs hinge
& lid lifts off base

to gift a bowl that over
brims.

Reverse wrist-twist
& meat is freed

to swim past lips toward
back of tongue—

but first: bite, burst,
your mouth is sluiced

with briny sweet of bay
& you jump in.

CAMOUFLAGE

The baboons piss on the concrete poured just last week,
scratch the smooth walls

into soften and crumble, working long into night. They will
not sleep, bellow, beat chest

or mate, or take any food until the etching is done —
template of tangled branch, trunk, and root,

template of template of memory, some stripe of sunrise
caught between branches, a monsoon-puddled

moon, orchids hung high in the tree canopy. They scrape
overhead until concrete passes for sky

in the wet season. Squat, piss, squat, piss again until the floor
smells grown, not laid. When the zoo

hunkers down in the afternoon heat, they sit and wait for dusk,
falling light, and the wind rising.

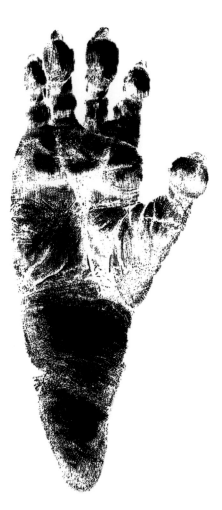

PERFECT

Mudflat mirror in mottled silver, mauve, five
shades of taupe. Air barrel-aged in live oak
and madrone. Phoenix Lake's green jewel.
Mule deer and the tufted bobcat. Roses

blooming straight through late fall. Hawthorn
leaves in drift, a child's sleep-flushed cheek.
Purple against orange: sage and maple.
Peonies under palms, cactus bristling

next to the fat pout of a pink hybrid tea.
Trout lilies and wild iris. Mt. Tam mantled
each dawn in fog, then naked and lit
from within. Winter sunsets, the sky a wound,

the sky vivid and gashed, each day
bound to the last with dark thread.

WHAT FOLLOWS

If a tree falls and no one hears,
then it didn't fall, you'd say, but
I say the tree would know it fell,

and so would the hive-world
that had hummed and teemed
in its leaves. And the flowers

would know, each sticky stamen
barren of pollen. *Okay,* you say,
then think of a rock

that fell, and I didn't hear it. Well,
I see earth's new crater, blades
of grass bent, dust disturbed;

each perturbed molecule knows
that rock fell. *Okay, so it happened,*
you'd say, *but not for me, not*

my reality if I didn't hear it or see it.
But I say my reality is one web
with strands that go everywhere

so that mine waste washed down
a river wafts its effluent plume
through estuary and ocean

linking endless land to endless
land I walk through, the air
I breathe in. I never even licked

that apple, but my heel still
is stung. With original sin,
it only begins.

STEWARD

Our hands reach for the plough and spade
to loosen the soil annealed by neglect,
but now is the season of sickle and blade.

When it was spring in this garden, we laid
plans for an orchard that bloomed in our lips
and our eyes. We took up the plough and spade

to pledge our troth with the earth. When did
we break that covenant? When, let lapse
the deed? They grew dull, our sickle and blade,

we failed to cut back the blight. Now we bleed,
bitten by the thorn of a rose in whose hips
are stored our silent poisons, and the plough

is slugged. Cut the cane's throat now, unbraid
the field from the bindweed, its twining clasp.
Song of water and whetstone on blade,

song of the scythe parting vines overhead.
Bees swarm to the light that warms a new glade,
but not here. Lay down your plough and spade
—quick, it's late! Sharpen your sickle and blade.

TAXONOMY

Kingdom, phylum,
class, order, family,
genus, species.
Each named thing
hooved or horned
or fragile-winged,
tawny-beaked
or forked-of-tongue.

We take note of it
and make our lists:
size and shape
of crest, pitch
and tone of trill,
spot, or not,
on tufted breast;
each beast wedged
into its slot,

each numbered song.

LAZARUS

And he that was dead came forth...
— John 11:44.

"I am Lazarus, come back from the dead. / Come back to tell you all..."
— T. S. Eliot, "The Love Song of J. Alfred Prufrock"

Arakan forest turtle. Armoured frog. Banggai crow. Bavarian pine vole. Bahia tapaculo. Berlepsch's parotia. Bermuda petrel. Blunt chaff flower. Brazilian arboreal mouse. Bruijn's brush-turkey. Café marron. Cebu flowerpecker. Canterbury knobbed weevil. Caspian pony. Central rock rat. Chacoan peccary. Climbing alsinidendron. Coelacanth. Cone-billed tanager. Cuban solendon. Dawn redwood. Dinosaur ant. Edwards pheasant. Fernandina rice rat. Flat-headed myotis. Forest owlet. Furbish's lousewort. Giant Palouse earthworm. Gilbert's potoroo. Golden-fronted bowerbird. Grand comoro scops-owl. Gray's monitor. Ivory-billed woodpecker. Jellyfish tree. Jerdon's courser. Kaempfer's woodpecker. La Gomera giant lizard. La Palma giant lizard. Laotian rock rat. Large-billed reed-warbler. Leadbeater's possum. Long-legged warbler. Lord Howe Island stick insect. Madagascar pochard. Madagascar serpent-eagle. Madeiran land snail. Mount Diablo buckwheat. Mountain pygmy possum. New Caledonian crested gecko. New Holland mouse. New Zealand longhorn beetle. New Zealand storm-petrel. Night parrot. Nightcap oak. Painted frog. Philippine bare-backed fruit bat. She cabbage tree. São Tomé fiscal. São Tomé grosbeak. Sicilian fir. Takahe. Stresemann's bristlefront. Tammar wallaby. Terror skink. Utila chachalaca. Virginia round-leaf birch. Wollemi pine. Woolly flying squirrel. Yellow-tailed woolly monkey.

SPRING WILL COME

Spring will come despite the rain—

mothwing petals sift past quince,
blooming bare-branched beneath
the plumed plum. Despite the rain,
despite the pain—or is it from,
or through? Prepositions don't matter

—spring will come.

PERENNIAL

When you've gone, it won't matter to the musk rose
twining the old trellis over the eaves. Willow
will continue to pour her yellow-green waterfall

next to forsythia, one half-tone better on the scale
of bright, and white jonquil spinnakers will sail
their acre of regatta

past hyssop's rising pale flower foam. It will
crest and subside and weave a sweet mat
to bear the thick blanket of snow,

and none of it matters. Not how you loved it, not
how you knelt in each dark December plot
to part the rich plait, reached

through the wither of winter to find something born
of the decay of all that was young once,
something still growing and green.

NOTES

God, Seed. The reference is to the Native American agrarian practice of planting seeds in mounds and using fish heads as fertilizer to renew the soil.

Lakemont Park and *Cricket at Play*. An amusement park in Altoona, Pennsylvania, Lakemont Park still operates "Leap the Dips," the oldest freestanding wooden roller coaster in the United States. *Cricket at Play* depicts a cricket in motion, using watercolor and lipstick fingerprints to dress the cricket in party clothes of grass and blossoms.

Mount Ellinor Hike. Mount Ellinor is in the Olympic Range in Washington state. Its summit experiences unexpected blizzards and provides a habitat for a population of feral mountain goats. *Mount Ellinor* is designed to resemble a postcard from the area.

Persimmon. In order to capture the sense of the immediacy and evanescence of the moment of perfect ripeness, this image was created in two brushstrokes: one for the fruit (orange) and one for the cap and stem (green). The process required many drafts, teaching the artist that when painting a persimmon a little too much yellow will yield an orange, and a bit too much red will produce a tomato.

Unheard. While large numbers of bison now exist in conservation herds, wild bison were hunted nearly to extinction in the nineteenth century. Some species of puffins are extinct, but others still thrive. "Of their bones are fossils made" is an allusion to Ariel's song in *The Tempest*. The italicized terms are from *An Exaltation of Larks* by James Lipton (Penguin 1993), a classic anthology of collective nouns establishing Lipton's "terms of venery" for the correct (or at least the cleverest) manner of referring to groups of animals and other nouns. Thanks to John Kessler for the gift of this wonderful book.

***Shell* and Fossil Record.** This is a rubbing of a fossil that, like the other fossils named, was collected by the author during childhood forays into the strip mines scarring the western Pennsylvania landscape in the 1960s.

Raystown River Trout. The italicized words are from Elizabeth Bishop's poem, "The Fish," and *mystery* and *glitter* recall Mary Oliver's poem by the same name.

Trout. An example of the traditional Japanese art of fish printing, this *gyotaku* print was achieved after much trial and error involving the artist visiting fishermen on the banks of Phoenix Lake in search of a whole specimen and in the end stuffing, sewing, and freezing a gutted fish.

Carp. For this painting, the artist is indebted to the California Academy of Sciences ichthyology collection of fish specimens in jars. A visitor wanting a closer look is provided with the jar, a tray, and a pair of tongs. Afterward, the jars are returned to the stacks and filed like books.

Nuclear. This poem was inspired by Bay Area poet Jack Foley's practice of writing "between the lines" of other poems. Most of the odd-numbered lines are from Vergil, *The Aeneid* 2.199–249, trans. David Ferry. *Literary Imagination* 10: 17–18 (2008). The italicized lines are from the *Bhagavad Gita*, a sacred Hindu scripture.

Day. On August 27, 2007, Native American poet Sherwin Bitsui and writer and third-generation Oregon rancher William Kittredge read at the Bread Loaf Writers' Conference, where Kittredge told a story about a rancher shooting magpies and using pesticides that devastated bird populations in lands once roamed by Native Americans.

Bee Fugue and *Honeycomb*. Colony Collapse Disorder is a phenomenon in which worker bees abruptly disappear from their hive. While such disappearances have occurred throughout the history of apiculture, the number of disappearances of North American honeybee colonies increased drastically in 2006. Besides the ecological impact, colony collapse is economically significant because so many agricultural crops are pollinated by bees. The different cell colorations in *Honeycomb* correspond to the function (honey storage, royal jelly storage, embryo incubation) performed by such cells.

Last Bison Gone. The huia bird, once a flourishing population in New Zealand, is now extinct. Huia mated for life, and the male and female of the species were adapted so as to make them reliant upon each other in order to eat; male huia had short, tough beaks for shredding bark while the females had long, curved beaks for extracting insects. Herds of wild bison are dwindling today. The bison in prehistoric cave drawings discovered on the walls of the caves in Lascaux, France, are in danger of extinction from lichens and other organisms proliferating since the caves were opened to visitors in the 1950s.

Huia Feather. This feather shows the banding pattern characteristic of the huia, a quality that made it highly desirable for specimen mounting and millinery use. What we have left of the huia is a great many stuffed birds, together with feathers adorning Victorian hatbands and brooches.

Seeds of the Giant Sequoia and *Pine Cone.* Fire plays a positive role in the life cycles of many forests, for example, by preparing a seedbed and promoting seed germination. See Bruce M. Kilgore, *Naturalist* 23(1): 26–37 (1972).

Baboon Footprint. This digital re-imagination of a drawing made by and used with the permission of Charles Wood was created by inverting the blacks and whites of the image to resemble the print of a wet foot.

Globe Head. This watercolor is of a sculpture made by the artist who cut the shape of a human head from a metal globe in order to represent the interrelation of humankind with nature. The negative space of the hole in the globe recalls the images in "Fossil Record."

Lazarus. A "Lazarus species" is an organism rediscovered alive after years of having been considered extinct.

Perennial. This plein air watercolor of perennial blossoms, made while the artist was on a picnic with friends in Minnesota, captures the essence of spontaneity. After making many subsequent versions in her studio, the artist decided to return to her first draft.

ACKNOWLEDGMENTS

Grateful acknowledgment is made to the following publications, in which some of the poems and art in this book first appeared, sometimes under a different title:

Ambush Review, The Antigonish Review, Atlanta Review, Bayou, Canary, Dos Passos Review, Flyway Journal, Fourteen Hills, Knock Journal, The Ledge, The Literary Bohemian, Many Mountains Moving Journal, Marin Poetry Center Anthology 2009, Mudlark, North American Review, Poetry East, Poets for Living Waters, Red Rock Review, Rosebud, Sand Hill Review, The Spoon River Poetry Review, Terrain, The Texas Review, Twelve Ways: IWL Anthology (Kearny Street Press), *Two Review, and West Marin Review.* Some poems also appeared in the chapbook *Mom's Canoe* (Texas Review Press) and in the book *All That Gorgeous Pitiless Song* (Many Mountains Moving Press).

Thanks to the following for their inspiration: Charles Wood (for *Baboon Footprint*), William Kittredge (for "Day"), Craig Challender (for "Steward"), and Mel Schorin (for "What Follows").

The following media were used to create the art in this book: *Cricket at Play*, watercolor and print; *Mount Ellinor*, watercolor; *Poppies*, watercolor; *Apple*, print; *Persimmon*, watercolor; *Persimmon Branch*, pencil; *Shell*, crayon rubbing with watercolor wash; *Trout*, print; *Carp*, watercolor; *Cormorant*, watercolor and acrylic; *Matrix*, watercolor; *Sighted*, pencil and watercolor; *Honeycomb*, gesso and watercolor; *Seep*, watercolor; *Crux*, charcoal rubbing; *Herd*, ink; *Huia Feather*, pencil; *Pine Cone*, watercolor; *Soar*, watercolor; *Wave*, watercolor with gum mask; *Baboon Footprint*, digital image; *Alpenglow*, watercolor and digital image; *Serpent*, watercolor and acrylic paint; *Globe Head*, watercolor on photograph; *Fern*, watercolor; *Garden*, watercolor.

ABOUT THE AUTHOR AND ARTIST

Rebecca Foust (left) and Lorna Stevens.

Rebecca Foust's book, *All That Gorgeous Pitiless Song*, won the 2008 Many Mountains Moving Book Award and was released in April 2010. Two chapbooks, *Mom's Canoe* and *Dark Card*, received the Robert Phillips Prize in 2007 and 2008. Foust's poems are in current or forthcoming issues of *Arts & Letters Journal, Margie, The North American Review, The Hudson Review, Spoon River Poetry Review,* and others.

Lorna Stevens received her MFA in sculpture from Columbia University. She exhibits widely in galleries and public spaces. Her work has been featured or reviewed in *The Boston Globe, The San Francisco Chronicle, The Marin Independent Journal,* and *Artweek* and has been acquired by the Brooklyn Museum, the New York Public Library, and the di Rosa Collection in Napa, California.